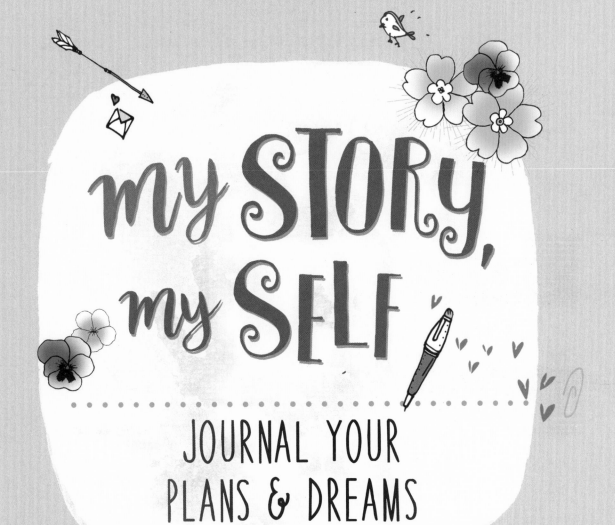

my STORY, my SELF

JOURNAL YOUR PLANS & DREAMS

Anna Brett

BARRON'S

How to Use This Journal

Don't live in a hand-me-down world of others' experiences — write about yours!

This journal is for you and about you! All you need to do is keep turning the pages for prompts, advice, and great tips.

YOU CAN RECORD IT ALL HERE: your habits, your achievements, your dreams, your hopes, and your fears. And at the end of it all you'll get a chance to see just how far you've come and what you've learned about YOU!

There are different styles of pages in this journal, and some of the key pages have been listed here so you can use them as a contents list and flip back and forth. Jot down any other pages that are important to you as you work through the book!

1. Some pages are quick and easy to fill in. Why not copy the ideas in a blank notebook so you can write more later. For example:

2. You'll also find tracker pages. They are pages you'll visit again and again to keep track of your habits, moods, and daily routine. You might choose to continue using these trackers if you want. For example:

3. Certain pages are packed with tips! They are full of handy hints and questions to give you insight into yourself and your surroundings. For example:

- 20–21 My Space
- 44–45 Yummy in my Tummy

4. The fourth page style you'll encounter are those you'll want to look back on in a week, a month, or even several years' time! These tell your story! For example:

- 10–11 Describe Me
- 36–37 My Future
- 66–67 The Playlists

My Cal

The year is yours!
What will you do with it?

Use this journal every day for an entire year! It doesn't matter where you start.

COLOR IN YOUR SQUARES ACCORDING TO THIS KEY:

YELLOW = a normal day: you feel content

PINK = something fabulous happened today: you feel happy

RED = an important event happened today: something to remember

GREEN = you tried something new today: you've got a buzz

BLUE = something made you sad or angry today: you're down but tomorrow is a new day!

January

1	2	3	4	5	6	7
8	9	10	11	12	13	14
15	16	17	18	19	20	21
22	23	24	25	26	27	28
29	30	31				

February

1	2	3	4	5	6	7
8	9	10	11	12	13	14
15	16	17	18	19	20	21
22	23	24	25	26	27	28
29						

March

1	2	3	4	5	6	7
8	9	10	11	12	13	14
15	16	17	18	19	20	21
22	23	24	25	26	27	28
29	30	31				

April

1	2	3	4	5	6	7
8	9	10	11	12	13	14
15	16	17	18	19	20	21
22	23	24	25	26	27	28
29	30					

May

1	2	3	4	5	6	7
8	9	10	11	12	13	14
15	16	17	18	19	20	21
22	23	24	25	26	27	28
29	30	31				

June

1	2	3	4	5	6	7
8	9	10	11	12	13	14
15	16	17	18	19	20	21
22	23	24	25	26	27	28
29	30					

July

1	2	3	4	5	6	7
8	9	10	11	12	13	14
15	16	17	18	19	20	21
22	23	24	25	26	27	28
29	30	31				

August

1	2	3	4	5	6	7
8	9	10	11	12	13	14
15	16	17	18	19	20	21
22	23	24	25	26	27	28
29	30	31				

September

1	2	3	4	5	6	7
8	9	10	11	12	13	14
15	16	17	18	19	20	21
22	23	24	25	26	27	28
29	30					

October

1	2	3	4	5	6	7
8	9	10	11	12	13	14
15	16	17	18	19	20	21
22	23	24	25	26	27	28
29	30	31				

November

1	2	3	4	5	6	7
8	9	10	11	12	13	14
15	16	17	18	19	20	21
22	23	24	25	26	27	28
29	30					

December

1	2	3	4	5	6	7
8	9	10	11	12	13	14
15	16	17	18	19	20	21
22	23	24	25	26	27	28
29	30	31				

What was your favorite month of the year?

– – – – – – – – – – –

All About Me

"Be yourself; everyone else is already taken." — OSCAR WILDE

CONGRATULATIONS! There's a new movie being released called *The Story of You*, and you've got the lead role!

Fill in this section with details about yourself and you'll find you've got the all the information about the star character right before your eyes.

The Story of You
CREDITS

Lead role (your name): . . . .

Release date (of birth): . . . .

Producers (your parents or guardians): . . . .

Supporting cast (siblings and friends): . . . .

Filmed on location at home in: . . . .

And in the school called: . . . .

Key quote of *The Story of You*: . . . .

This Is me!

Check out your private, offline profile page – the only person who can comment on it is YOU!

Choose your **THREE** favorite colors to fill in your perfect profile in a super-stylish way.

HAIR COLOR:

- ☐ blonde
- ☐ brown
- ☐ ginger
- ☐ black
- ☐ other

I look like this:
(Doodle yourself)

EYE COLOR:

☐ blue ☐ brown ☐ green
☐ gray ☐ other: ....

Three words that describe me:

1. ....
2. ....
3. ....

Height:

☐ shorter than friends

☐ average among friends

☐ taller than friends

FAVORITE COLOR:

. . . .

Favorite subject
at school:

. . . .

Today I Feel:

HAPPY   SAD

Relaxed

Anxious

HEALTHY

Athletic

Bored

CRAZY   Sassy

Favorite movie: . . . .

Favorite book: . . . .

Favorite place: . . . .

Favorite song: . . . .

I'D DESCRIBE MY STYLE AS:

☐ sporty   ☐ geek-chic   ☐ laid-back

☐ trendy   ☐ party   ☐ other: . . . .

Describe Me

Write your name here

....

and then write down the
words that best describe you.

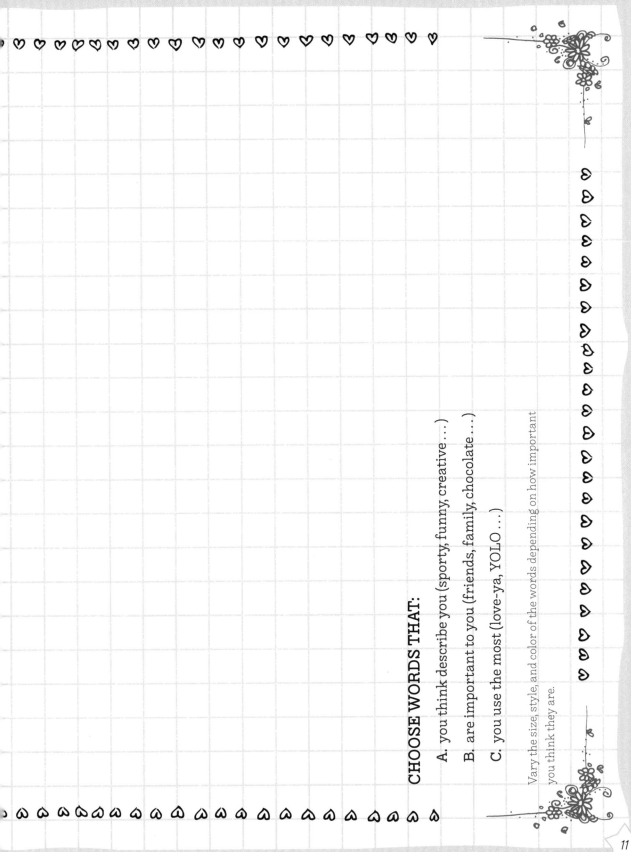

CHOOSE WORDS THAT:

A. you think describe you (sporty, funny, creative . . .)

B. are important to you (friends, family, chocolate . . .)

C. you use the most (love-ya, YOLO . . .)

Vary the size, style, and color of the words depending on how important you think they are.

A Snapshot of Today

Today might turn out to be one of the best days of your life! Whatever happens, you'll always have a reminder of this day as a written memory. You can do this at various points in your life and see how things change.

DATE:

M T W T F S S (CIRCLE THE DAY)

I woke up at

. . . .

I WENT TO . . . .

. . . .

I wore . . . .

. . . .

. . . .

. . . .

I MET . . . .

. . . .

. . . .

. . . .

Breakfast: . . . .

Lunch: . . . .

Dinner: . . . .

Snacks: . . . .

Best thing today:

....

....

....

....

WORST THING TODAY:

....

....

....

....

I WENT TO BED AT: ....

FUN AND GAMES TODAY:

• ....

• ....

• ....

Quote of the day: ....

....

....

....

BEST PART:

....

....

....

....

....

....

....

Routine Tracker

USE THIS GRID to track your routine over two weeks. Shade or write in the squares using a different color for each line.

WEEK ONE	MON	TUES	WEDS	THURS	FRI	SAT	SUN	TOTALS
Wake-up time								
Slept for at least eight hours – Y or N?								
Time watching TV								
Time chatting to friends								
Time doing homework								
Portions of fruit and veg								
Glasses of water drunk								
Read a book – Y or N?								
Time spent outdoors – Y or N?								
Helped someone – Y or N?								

Surprised by the results? Would you change anything?

"Every moment is a fresh beginning." – T. S. ELIOT

WEEK TWO	MON	TUES	WEDS	THURS	FRI	SAT	SUN	TOTALS
Wake-up time								
Slept for at least eight hours – Y or N?								
Time watching TV								
Time chatting to friends								
Time doing homework								
Portions of fruit and veg								
Glasses of water drunk								
Read a book – Y or N?								
Time spent outdoors – Y or N?								
Helped someone – Y or N?								

If you wanted to change something, did you? ....

15

Mix It Up

Which of your routines would you like to change? Pick one and create a grid telling yourself how to achieve it. If you wanted to get up earlier, for example, you could make yourself a list like the one below and try one method each day.

Now write down what you'd like to do differently and invent your own change chart.

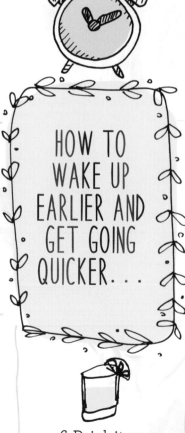

HOW TO WAKE UP EARLIER AND GET GOING QUICKER . . .

1. Personal stylist – put your clothes out the night before.

2. Motivate me – write down the thing you're most looking forward to tomorrow before you go to sleep.

3. Change the tune – pick a different sound for your alarm clock or ask your Mom to wake you up with a tune.

4. Say no to the snooze – put your alarm clock on the other side of the room.

5. Let there be light – open the curtains and let in the natural light.

6. Drink it up – gulp down a glass of lemon water.

7. Stretch session – do five minutes of yoga as soon as you get out of bed.

What worked for you?

Sleep Style

Deep sleep or restless dreams? Answer these questions to discover your sleep style and see what it means.

1 WHAT DO YOU WEAR TO GO TO BED?

A. Clean, fresh pajamas

B. Whatever pajamas you can find

C. That big baggy t-shirt you also wear around the house

2 WHAT IS YOUR BED LIKE WHEN YOU JUMP INTO IT?

A. Neatly made

B. Exactly as when I got out of it in the morning

C. Covered in books, technology, homework, and clothes

3 HOW DO YOU FALL ASLEEP?

A. On your back

B. On your side

C. On your front

4 HOW DO YOU FEEL WHEN YOU WAKE UP?

A. Hey, it's a brand new day!

B. OK, I guess

C. Oh no, is it that time already?

5 HOW OFTEN DO YOU WAKE UP IN THE NIGHT?

A. Never

B. Once

C. More than once

6 WHEN DO YOU FALL ASLEEP?

A. Roughly the same time each night

B. It depends what I've been doing

C. Whenever I feel like it

7 DO YOU LEAVE YOUR PHONE OR TABLET ON YOUR BEDSIDE TABLE?

A. No, I need my sleep!

B. Yes, but in silent mode

C. Yes, I don't want to miss anything

Mostly As = You're most likely a good sleeper because you don't let anything get in the way of your shut-eye time. Your bed is saved for its one important job – helping you sleep! Don't go changing it.

Mostly Bs = You're not doing too badly, but you're sure to have a few difficult nights because you're not making sleep as enjoyable as it could be. Make your bed and treat yourself to some new pajamas and you'll look forward to going to bed.

Mostly Cs = Uh-oh, you're likely a bad sleeper! Your bed is behaving more like a desk! Think of bedtime as different to the rest of the day and change your routine to match it.

Plan your ideal bedtime routine here and try to stick to it!

BEFORE BED I WILL: . . . .

MY BED WILL BE: . . . .

I WILL ALWAYS: . . . .

My Space

Whether you have a bedroom to yourself or share it, think about the space you have. Does it really reflect who you are … or is it who you were a year ago … or even worse, nothing to do with your personality at all?

List personal or decorative items in your space and review their purpose! Decide if you really need them or if you should throw them out or upgrade them.

Remember, it's fine to keep things you love, even if they don't have a purpose!

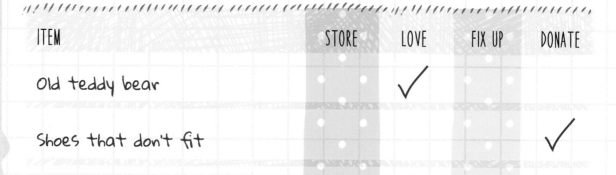

ITEM	STORE	LOVE	FIX UP	DONATE
Old teddy bear		✓		
Shoes that don't fit				✓

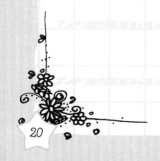

ITEM	STORE	LOVE	FIX UP	DONATE

Ask your parents about donating things you don't use!

My Dream Room

Design dream it, then design do it! Doodle parts of your dream perfect bedroom on these pages. Imagine you can do anything you like! Then take a look at your ideas. Could you make them happen in real life? Talk to your parents about what you could do to achieve them.

Choose

- Colors
- Work zone
- Relax zone
- Friend zone
- Sleep zone

Here is some help for how to design your room!

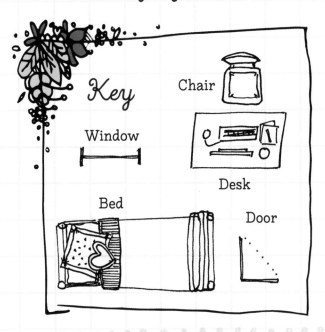

Key

Chair

Window

Desk

Bed

Door

Get on the Hobbyhorse

What do you love to do outside of school? Is it sports, crafts, reading, singing? Here's a space to think about what you have done, what you do at the moment, and what you dream of doing.

List all the activities you've done in the past couple of years. Underline the ones you really loved.

FUN WITH FRIENDS:

EXPRESSING MYSELF:

NEW EXPERIENCES:

Keeping active:

IN THE NEXT MONTH,
I WILL TRY FOR THE
FIRST TIME:

In the next
year, I want
to achieve:

WHEN I GROW UP, I'D LOVE TO
MAKE THIS HOBBY MY CAREER:

Spirit Animal

Whether you're a creature lover or not, everyone has an animal spirit inside them! Find yours and it will help guide you through life.

1 I'D SAY I'M:

A. Down-to-earth

B. Head in the clouds

C. Cool and calm

D. Hot-headed

2 I THINK I:

A. Am an easy listener

B. Think before I speak

C. Can talk to anyone

D. Am a chatterbox

3 DAY TO DAY:

A. I like routine

B. I never know what's next

C. I'm happy to go with the flow

D. I do what I want when I want

4 I'M MOST HAPPY WHEN:

A. I'm with my family

B. I'm on my own

C. I'm surrounded by my friends

D. I meet new people

5 I LIKE OTHERS TO:

A. Hug and support me

B. Let me have space

C. Help me experience new things

D. Not get in my way but follow me

6 A PERFECT DAY WOULD BE:

A. Games in the park

B. Reading my favorite book

C. Playing sports

D. Doing something new and creative

Mostly As = Bear

Having a bear as a spirit animal gives you **strength** and acts as a grounding force in your life. These big creatures give you **courage** to be who you are, which includes offering **support** to others. They are social creatures, warm and **cuddly,** and will always be there to keep you strong and focused.

Mostly Bs = Eagle

Having an eagle as a spirit animal means people will see you as **sensible** and **wise.** An eagle allows you to rise above any problems and think outside the box for solutions. Eagles are solitary creatures; this means they can react quickly to what is happening around them so your spirit eagle will be a great guide throughout your life.

Mostly Cs = Dolphin

Dolphin spirit animals are **playful, friendly,** and allow you to be a great friend to others and create **harmony** in a group. Dolphins pass on their energy to you and so you're likely to be good at **sports.** You'll always look on the bright side of life and not be afraid to try new things with a dolphin by your side.

Mostly Ds = Fox

The fox spirit animal is the **leader** of the pack and will help you to be a leader, too. With a fox by your side, you can be wild and **unpredictable,** but people respect you as you make your own path and are very loyal. All this energy means lots of **creative** ideas will come your way.

The traits I share with my spirit animal are: . . . .

My Happy Month

A journal is the perfect place for you to think, feel, discover, expand, remember, and dream.

Write down one or two sentences every day to record something that made you happy, something new you discovered or a great idea that you want to remember.

DATE   WHAT MADE ME SMILE TODAY

My Year: Part One

Look back over the year that you've had and plan ahead. Think about your next six months on these pages and the six months after that on the next two pages. You can add important events, plans, and goals – anything you like!

Write the name of the month at the top of each box and use it to plan, plot, and dream. Goals may include:

- Volunteering during school holidays
- Cutting down on TV time
- Trying three new foods
- Making a new friend

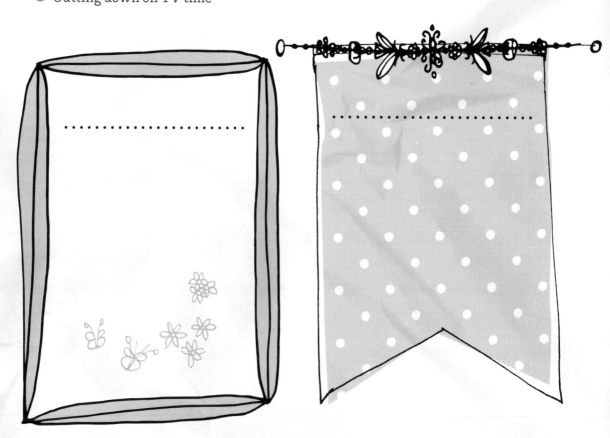

. . . .

. . . .

My Year: Part Two

Return to these pages whenever you want to see if you've achieved your goals!

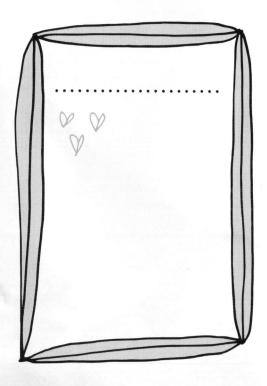

My Memories

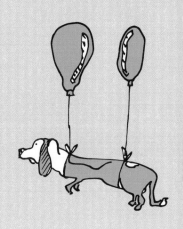

"Things end, but memories last forever."

– KUMAR MILAN

Some memories, though, have a tendency to float away until something reminds you. Fill in these pages over the life of this journal.

Memories you want to make sure you always remember.

My Future

Where do you see yourself in 5 years, 10 years, 20, and 30 years? Write down whatever you most wish for and then set yourself on the path to achieve it!

In 5 years:

I'll be ...... years old

I will be ....

....

....

In 10 years:

I'll be ...... years old

I will be ....

....

....

In 20 years:

I'll be ...... years old
I will be ....
....
....

In 30 years:

I'll be ......
years old
I will be ....

....
....
....
....
....

My Well-being

"Health is a state of body. Wellness is a state of being." — J. STANFORD

This is all about your physical and mental **health** — when you work on both you'll feel your very best!

Positive thoughts

Positive vibes

Positive life

The Power of Positivity

Whatever happens, try to see the **POSITIVE** in everything and you'll be a happier, more successful person!
You are what you think, not what others think of you.

> " IF YOU HAVE GOOD THOUGHTS THEY WILL SHINE OUT OF YOUR FACE LIKE SUNBEAMS AND YOU WILL ALWAYS LOOK LOVELY. " — *THE TWITS*, ROALD DAHL

YOU CAN EASILY TRAIN YOURSELF TO BE A POSITIVE PERSON.

Start by writing down three good things that happened today (they can be as big or small as you like):

1 _____

2 _____

3 _____

Continue to do this at the end of every day!

What are you most looking forward to about tomorrow?

_____

_____

Think of a way you can be kind to someone and do it tomorrow!

_____

_____

TURN THAT FROWN UPSIDE DOWN.

Challenge yourself to turn that frown upside down when something bad happens. Here are three ways to tackle the blues.

1 Make a joke out of it. Laughter lightens most loads.

2 Spend some time with your friends and family, or plan a fun activity for the future. You'll feel better in no time!

3 Try to see the problem from the bright side. Could it lead to something more positive in the future?

YOUR MOOD TRACKER

Spend a month tracking your days! Add any other categories below that you think might affect your mood, and see if they match up!

MONTH _____

	WONDERFUL DAY	GOOD DAY	NORMAL DAY	BAD DAY	EXERCISE/ PLAYING SPORTS	FUN WITH FRIENDS	CHILLING OUT	EXAM
1								
2								
3								
4								
5								
6								
7								
8								
9								
10								
11								
12								
13								
14								
15								
16								
17								
18								
19								
20								
21								
22								
23								
24								
25								
26								
27								
28								
29								
30								
31								

Wonderful Words

"*Let your smile change the world, but don't let the world change your smile.*"
– CONNOR FRANTA

A great way to help you be at your best is to surround yourself with motivational quotes. These will remind you that anything is possible and put a smile on your face!

When you're having trouble with friends:

"Spread love everywhere you go. Let no one ever come to you without leaving happier."

Mother Teresa

When you're feeling stuck with a problem you can't solve:

"Think left and think right and think low and think high. Oh, the thinks you can think up if only you try!"

Dr. Seuss

When you're worried about the future:

"We do not need magic to change the world. We carry all the power we need inside ourselves already."

J. K. Rowling

When you're feeling like school is a waste of time:

"One child, one teacher, one book, one pen can change the world."

Malala Yousafzai

When you're having a wardrobe crisis:

"Happiness and confidence are the prettiest things you can wear."

Taylor Swift

Ask your family and friends for their favorite positive messages and write them down here.

Try different styles of writing to make each quote stand out.

Keep a list of sayings that inspire you whenever you read them.

Yummy in My Tummy

We all need food that tastes great and makes us feel good! Plan out your perfect food and drink line-up for a day.

Can you describe what it is that makes each bite great? Is it that sweet taste, or maybe it's only delicious the way someone cooks it? Perhaps you prefer foods that are soft and squishy, or maybe those that pack a crunch?

BREAKFAST I can't wait to wake my taste buds up with:

....

Because ....

....

LUNCH My favorite food for lunch is:

....

Because ....

....

DINNER I love to feast on:

. . . .

Because . . . .

. . . .

TREATS My naughty but nice treat to eat is:

. . . .

Because . . . .

. . . .

MY HEALTHY OPTION to gobble down when I'm having a break is:

. . . .

Because . . . .

. . . .

DRINKS Glug, glug, glug — the best thirst quencher is:

. . . .

Because . . . .

. . . .

Come Dine With Me

Pretend it's your birthday and you are having your friends over for a fancy meal. What will be on the menu?

Menu

Upon arrival, guests will be served this appetizer:

. . . .

Salad will be offered before dinner:

. . . .

The main dish will be:

. . . .

For sides, we'll have:

. . . .

♥ ♥ ♥ ♥ ♥ ♥ ♥ ♥ ♥ ♥ ♥

To finish, dessert will be:

. . . .

Throughout the evening,
these drinks will be offered:

. . . .

♥ ♥ ♥ ♥ ♥ ♥ ♥ ♥ ♥ ♥ ♥

If people have space
for a late-night snack,
they can enjoy:

. . . .

Move to the Beat!

It's a fact that exercising makes you feel better. It's time to get moving!

But rather than literally just jumping up and down in place (yawn!), grab a friend (or maybe your dog could watch!) and get some music playing. Plan fun ways of moving your body to different songs.

Let the music flow through your arms and legs and then write down or draw your routine here.

SONG	MOVES

SONG   MOVES

Listen to the beat and see if it's fast or slow, crazy, or calm. Are parts of the song different than others? But don't overdo it with your moves! You're aiming to be a little out of breath by the end, but still able to chat to a friend/ your dog.

Gold Star

Award a gold star to your favorite dance!

Team Player or Solo Star

An easy way to get more exercise in your life is to take up a sport. There are loads of things you can do as a team or an individual. Which one will you join?

Answer these questions to guide you toward a new sport:

TEAM

E.g. soccer, football, hockey, cheerleading, basketball, softball, water polo.

Join a team and you'll make new friends just by showing up. It doesn't matter if you've never tried the sport before; just give it a try and your teammates will support you. Even if you're the worst player on the team, your teammates may still lead you to victory!

INDIVIDUAL

E.g. swimming, cycling, gymnastics, equestrian, tennis, dance.

Take up an individual sport and your efforts will lead directly to your success! Individual sports allow you to set the standard and just by practicing you'll improve in no time. Achieving new personal bests is the greatest reward! But make sure you set aside time for training; just like you would with a team sport.

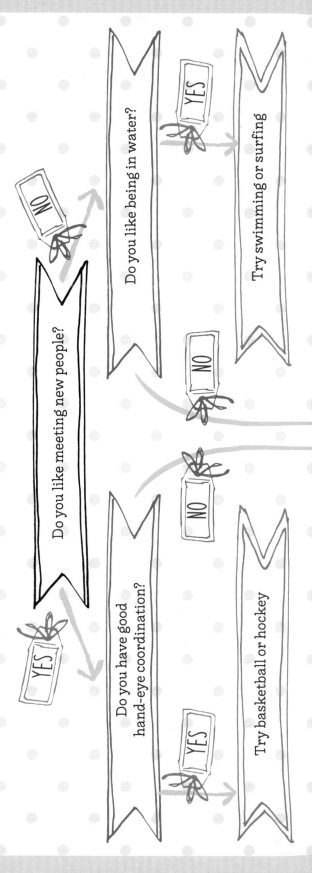

Do you like meeting new people?

YES
Do you have good hand-eye coordination?

YES
Try basketball or hockey

NO
Do you like being in water?

YES
Try swimming or surfing

NO

ON

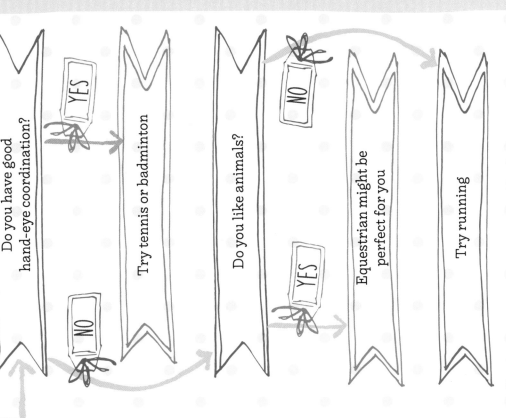

Do you have good hand-eye coordination?

YES → Try tennis or badminton

NO →

Do you like animals?

YES → Equestrian might be perfect for you

NO → Try running

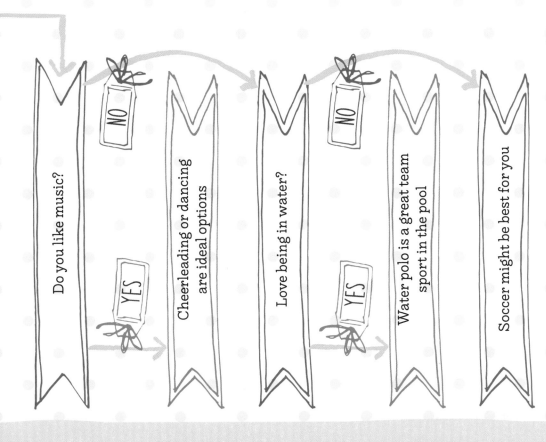

Do you like music?

YES → Cheerleading or dancing are ideal options

NO →

Love being in water?

YES → Water polo is a great team sport in the pool

NO → Soccer might be best for you

If you really hate the idea of sports but want to be part of a team, what about learning to become an umpire or a team trainer?

You'll end up enjoying your time to yourself and getting fit in the process!

Back to Basics

Imagine your great grandparents (bonus points if you know their names!) **when they were your age.**

Think of some of the things they might have done, then see if you can get back to basics and experience them all in a week.

Here are some to get you started. Check them off once you've completed them. How many did you really enjoy? Continue to include them in your regular daily routine!

☐ Close your eyes and breathe deeply . . . in and out . . . for two minutes. It might sound silly, but with less technology to distract them, your distant relatives probably had a lot more calm, quiet time back then!

☐ Drink a glass of lemon water. There weren't many options other than water and milk for children to drink back in the old days, so see if you can get back to basics for a week.

☐ Sit outside for ten minutes without your phone – just enjoy the natural world. Over 100 years ago, the world had no TV or computers to keep people inside. Your great-grandparents probably spent more time outdoors than you do!

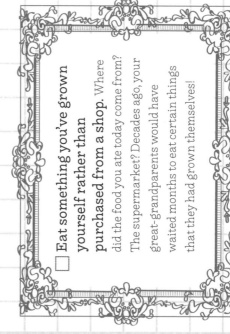

☐ Eat something you've grown yourself rather than purchased from a shop. Where did the food you ate today come from? The supermarket? Decades ago, your great-grandparents would have waited months to eat certain things that they had grown themselves!

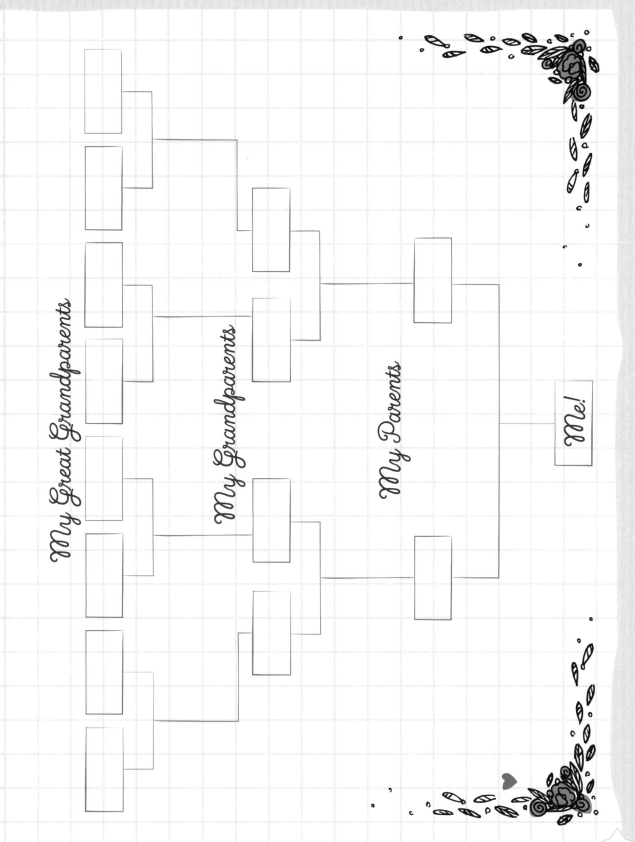

My Great Grandparents

My Grandparents

My Parents

Me!

Get Your Stretch On

Ever wondered why cats and dogs stretch so much? Because it feels sooo good! Give this stretch routine a try and you'll be purring like a cat in no time.

Only hold poses for as long as is comfortable – just feel a gentle stretch, don't force anything – and move slowly and thoughtfully. The more you do it, the easier it'll become.

First, make sure you don't do this routine on a full stomach! Then find somewhere with plenty of room to stretch out (check that it's OK to use the space).

1. Stand with your feet touching and arms down by your side. Breathe deeply and then slowly raise your arms up to the sky. Hold for ten seconds.

2. Take a deep breath then exhale slowly and bend forward to touch your toes. It's OK if you need to bend your knees a little.

3. Lift your right leg up and take a step back, away from your body. Place your hands flat on the floor. Bring your left leg back to line up with the right. Keep your hands on the floor.

4. Lift your hips up to create an upside-down V shape with your body. Hold for ten seconds, or for as long as is comfortable.

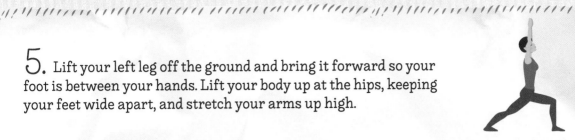

5. Lift your left leg off the ground and bring it forward so your foot is between your hands. Lift your body up at the hips, keeping your feet wide apart, and stretch your arms up high.

6. Twist your body and back foot to the right and point your left hand forward over your left leg and your right hand backward over your right leg. Look forward and hold for ten seconds.

7. Twist your body and back foot to face forward, then raise both arms above your head and point your fingertips up to the sky. Breathe deeply and count to ten.

8. Bring both hands down to the ground, place them on either side of your left foot, shoulder-width apart. Move your left leg back and then bring your body down to lay flat on the floor.

9. Bend the top half of your body up, with your weight pressing down through your hands.

10. Lower yourself gently back down into a flat position, then lift your hips to the sky and flex your feet forward again and do the upside-down V pose.

11. Shuffle your hands back toward your feet and then slowly lift your upper body up until you are back in a standing position. Stand perfectly still for ten seconds and concentrate on your breathing. Hopefully it feels like you've given your body a good cat-stretch!

My Perfect Chill Evening

Tune out. Turn off. Take some time to relax.
Allow your body and mind to switch off and
chill out every now and then with an evening
of "you time."

1 WHAT ARE YOUR FAVORITE WAYS TO RELAX?
Make a list of your top "you time" activities.

_____

_____

_____

_____

_____

_____

Here are a couple more ideas.
Check the ones you enjoy.

☐ DIY manicure

☐ drawing or painting

☐ watching a funny movie

☐ bubble bath

☐ reading a book

2 PLAN IT
Now schedule in your next chill-out
evening. Write the day and date of your
next chill-out evening here:

_____

_____

Take time to prepare your evening, and
make sure you don't plan too much.
Pick two or three activities from your
"you time" list you'd like to do.

1 _____

2 _____

3 _____

3 TOP TIPS

1 Tell family and friends about your evening to make sure they **don't interrupt you.**

2 Pick a song or poem that makes you feel good and play or read this at the start of your relax time. It'll get your head in the zone!

3 Try having some no-screen time at the start or end of your evening, and switch off your phone.

4 PREP YOUR CHILL ZONE

Before you start your perfect chill-out evening, tidy up the area to make the space around you cozy and calming, with no harsh lights or too much clutter. Make a list of everything you'll need to help you chill and gather it all in advance.

Here are a few more ideas for your chill area. Check the objects you'd like to have ready.

- **candles** (never leave a candle unattended and make sure to ask a grown-up before you light one!)

- **relaxing music** (take a look on pages 66–67 to find your playlists)

- a **warm blanket**

- a cup of **herbal tea**

1 _____

2 _____

3 _____

4 _____

5 _____

Heaven Scents

Don't you just love the smell of fresh cut grass? What about coming home to cookies straight out of the oven? There are so many amazing smells — write down the ones you love here.

LIP BALM IN THIS FLAVOR SMELLS THE BEST:
....

Do you prefer the smell of sunscreen or moisturizer:
....

THE BEST-SMELLING BUBBLE BATH IS:
....

MY FAVE shampoo SMELL IS:
....

MY FAVORITE SMELL AT SCHOOL IS:

My favorite

COOKING SMELL IS:

. . . .

MY FAVORITE FRUIT SMELL IS:

. . . .

Flowers that smell
the strongest are:

. . . .

Nifty Nails and Lovely Lips

It's fun and easy to look after your nails and lips. Show off your personality by what you wear on them, too!

Lips in sync

Here are some top tips for flawless lips!

1. Use lip balm to protect your lips from getting dry.

2. Gently rub them with a toothbrush to exfoliate.

3. Apply lip balm within the natural shape of your lips. Don't smear it all over your skin.

4. Pick a lip gloss color that suits your skin tone.

5. Go for a shade in your fave color for a fun look on the weekend.

6. Pick a product with a juicy smell to make those lips smile!

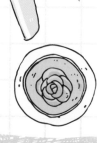

LIP BALM IS SOOTHING AND SCENTED.

LIP GLOSS WILL ADD SOME SHINE.

LIPSTICK IS MADE TO CREATE A COLOR POP.

Nurture your nails

Look after your nails — you have to look at them every day anyway!

1. Don't bite or chew them!

2. Moisturize your hands, fingers, and cuticles.

3. Keep them filed so sharp, jagged edges don't catch your clothes. Only file in one direction, though.

4. Nails are always growing, so you can have fun and create different shapes and lengths to match your mood each week.

5. Apply a clear polish before adding bright varnish to stop any staining.

6. Create nail art by using a second color, or apply glitter or stickers.

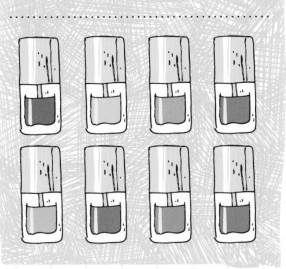

WHICH OF THESE COLORS ARE YOUR FAVORITE?

SMEAR A BLOB OF YOUR FAVORITE LIP PRODUCTS HERE AND MAKE NOTES ABOUT THEM.

Cozy on Up

You know that feeling you get when it's cold and rainy outside and you're snuggled inside on the sofa with a blanket, a candle, and a hot chocolate? Your body and mind are happy and at ease. Ahhhh...

But it doesn't always have to be lousy outside to get that great feeling inside!

Plan to get cozy for an hour, and prep according to these four areas:

1. ATMOSPHERE

Turn off that overhead light and use lamps and fairy lights to set the mood. Put on some chill-out music in the background and grab a book or magazine to read. If you can, spray some soft scents around the room. Lavender, cinnamon, and vanilla are great, or just pick some fresh flowers and put them in a vase near you.

Write down which items make you feel relaxed:

- . . . .
- . . . .
- . . . .

2. ENJOY THE MOMENT

A key part of feeling cozy is being present in the moment. This means no technology to distract you – turn that phone off! Set aside a period of time where you promise not to think about school, homework, exams, or gossip. Just enjoy the moment.

I'm going to switch my phone off for this amount of time during my cozy hour:

. . . .

3. COMFORT

One of the best parts about feeling cozy is getting comfortable. Put on your fluffy pajamas, wrap up in a cozy blanket, slip on some chunky socks, grab your favorite cuddly toy, and you'll have checked the comfort box. Give your insides some comfort, too, with your favorite treats and a hot drink.

Comfort items collected for my cozy hour:

- . . . .
- . . . .
- . . . .

4. HAPPY AND GRATEFUL

The final part of feeling cozy and relaxed is being thankful for what you have and forgetting any arguments or annoyances. There's a time and a place to be competitive, argumentative, or wishing things could change — but it's not now! Enjoy your home and know your friends and family are around you.

Things I am grateful for:

- . . . .
- . . . .
- . . . .

She Loves to Read

Do you love to read? Fill in the spines of these books to complete the library of your dreams!

MY FAVORITE BOOKS

BOOKS TO READ

BOOKS FOR SCHOOL

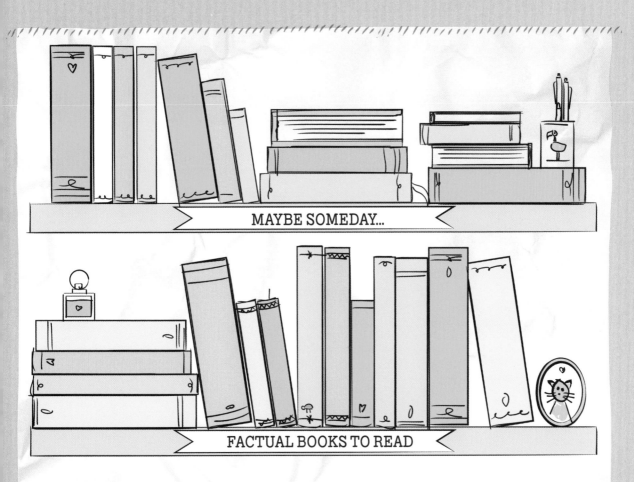

MAYBE SOMEDAY...

FACTUAL BOOKS TO READ

"You can find magic wherever you look.
Sit back and relax, all you need is a book."

– DR. SEUSS

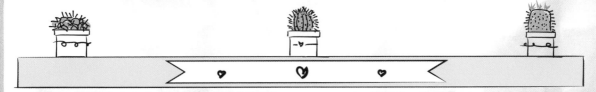

The Playlists

Make sure you have a special soundtrack for whatever each day brings. Write down your favorite songs in each category!

You can now start to use this as a music diary. Every time you hear a new song that you love, make a note of it here along with the date.

Party: Date:

Relax: Date:

Happy: Date:

My favorite song today:

Angry: Date:

Motivation: Date:

Study: Date:

Exercise: Date:

Give a Little

Spread some joy by giving to others. Write down ways you can put a smile on someone else's face — it's sure to make you smile, too!

WRITE DOWN THREE WAYS THAT YOU CAN HELP THOSE WHO ARE IN NEED

1

2

3

WRITE DOWN THREE WAYS YOU CAN HELP MAKE PEOPLE AT HOME SMILE

1

2

3

WRITE DOWN THREE WAYS YOU CAN BRING HAPPINESS TO PEOPLE AT SCHOOL

1 _____

2 _____

3 _____

WRITE DOWN WHEN SOMEONE DOES SOMETHING THAT PUTS
A SMILE ON YOUR FACE AND THEN THANK THEM FOR IT

1 _____

2 _____

3 _____

WRITE A LIST OF TEN PEOPLE YOU ARE GRATEFUL FOR IN YOUR LIFE — THEN TELL THEM!

1 _____   6 _____

2 _____   7 _____

3 _____   8 _____

4 _____   9 _____

5 _____   10 _____

Mood Tracker

Track your moods and feelings for the next four weeks. Draw an emoji face to show how you felt at each stage of the day. Then write a sentence about each day but focus on different things for the four weeks.

WEEK ONE	TODAY I FELT	MORNING	MIDDAY	AFTERNOON	EVENING
Monday					
Tuesday					
Wednesday					
Thursday					
Friday					
Saturday					
Sunday					

WEEK TWO	MOST LOOKING FORWARD TO	MORNING	MIDDAY	AFTERNOON	EVENING
Monday					
Tuesday					
Wednesday					
Thursday					
Friday					
Saturday					
Sunday					

> **"THE PURPOSE OF LIFE IS TO BE HAPPY."** — DALAI LAMA

WEEK THREE	BEST THING	MORNING	MIDDAY	AFTERNOON	EVENING
Monday					
Tuesday					
Wednesday					
Thursday					
Friday					
Saturday					
Sunday					

WEEK FOUR	I'M GRATEFUL FOR	MORNING	MIDDAY	AFTERNOON	EVENING
Monday					
Tuesday					
Wednesday					
Thursday					
Friday					
Saturday					
Sunday					

Doodle Delights

Every time you feel sad, worried, or angry, imagine all your concerns are trapped inside one of these circles and turn them into something happy — a shining sun, a smiley face, a gold medal, a flower — whatever you want!

When you turn back to these pages, you won't remember the bad things inside the circle, you'll just see happy doodles.

"You can't have a rainbow without a little rain!" – ANON

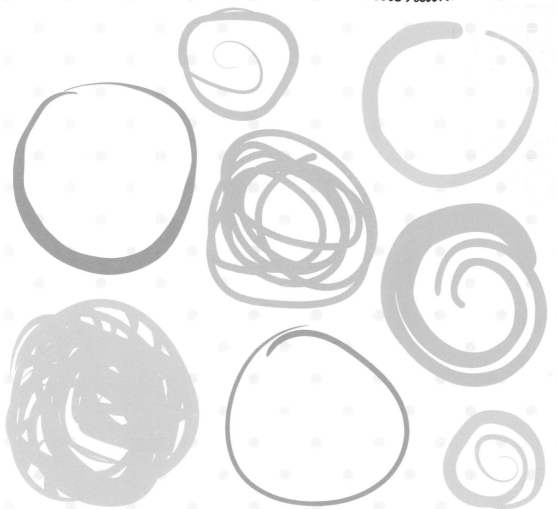

Dreaming Big

"If you can dream it, you can do it."
— WALT DISNEY

The future is yours for the taking — believe that you can do whatever you set out to achieve!

In this section, you should take the time to review your accomplishments up to now, then set yourself some goals for the coming year that will allow you to take a few steps toward your dreams!

In the future, I'd love to . . .

My dream job is:

· ·

My dream vacation is:

· ·

My dream home would be:

· ·

My favorite item to carry with me everywhere would be:

· ·

Dream Daze

What you dream about when you're asleep might give you clues to your deepest wishes and worries. Or might make no sense at all!

Track your dreams here...

DATE	DREAM	WHAT I THINK IT MEANS

DATE	DREAM	WHAT I THINK IT MEANS

"For in our dreams we enter a world that is entirely our own."

– ALBUS DUMBLEDORE
in *Harry Potter and the Prisoner of Azkaban*. J. K. Rowling.

Welcome to the Year 20__!

Plan your life five years from now!
Where would you like to be? Who will
be your friends? What are your goals?
Dream ahead and write it all down here.

WHAT WILL MY
STYLE BE LIKE?

WILL I HAVE A SPECIAL
PERSON IN MY LIFE?

HOW WILL I DO
IN SCHOOL?

WHAT WILL
I DO FOR FUN?

WHAT WILL MY
ROOM LOOK LIKE?

WHAT WILL BE MY SPECIAL
GOALS FOR THE FUTURE?

WHO WILL
BE MY FRIENDS?

New Day Resolutions

Never mind waiting until the new year to make your resolutions. If you want to achieve your dreams, then you should put yourself on the path to achieve them now!

My resolutions

TOMORROW:

1
2
3

NEXT WEEK:

1
2
3

NEXT MONTH:

1
2
3

THIS YEAR:

1 _____
2 _____
3 _____

NEXT YEAR:

1 _____
2 _____
3 _____

EVERY DAY I WILL:

_____
_____
_____
_____
_____
_____

THE MOST IMPORTANT THING
IN MY LIFE IS:

I WILL BE GRATEFUL FOR:

_____
_____
_____
_____
_____
_____

I WILL NEVER
FORGET THAT:

I PROMISE MYSELF
THAT I:

THE PEOPLE WHO
WILL HELP ME ARE:

WHEN SOMETHING
GOES WRONG, I WILL:

Would You Rather...?

A fun way to find out more about your likes, dislikes, and personal tastes is to answer these quick-fire questions.

Read the questions and then answer with the first thing that comes into your mind. There are no "right" or "wrong" answers, but you might be surprised by some of your responses!

WOULD YOU RATHER BE A FLOWER OR A TREE?

WOULD YOU RATHER ACT IN A SILLY COMEDY OR A SERIOUS DRAMA?

WOULD YOU RATHER FLY LIKE A BIRD OR SWIM LIKE A DOLPHIN?

WOULD YOU RATHER BE THE SMARTEST KID IN SCHOOL OR THE MOST ATHLETIC KID IN SCHOOL?

_____

_____

_____

WOULD YOU RATHER BE FAMOUS FOR YOUR DANCING OR YOUR SINGING?

Would you rather wear all red or all blue?

WOULD YOU RATHER TRAVEL 100 YEARS INTO THE FUTURE OR 100 YEARS INTO THE PAST?

_____
_____
_____

WOULD YOU RATHER SPEND THE REST OF YOUR LIFE OUTSIDE OR THE REST OF YOUR LIFE INSIDE?

_____
_____
_____

WOULD YOU RATHER EAT A BOILED EGG OR A SCRAMBLED EGG?

_____
_____
_____

WOULD YOU RATHER BE A PUPPY OR A KITTEN?

_____
_____
_____

Ask your friends and family to write down some more "would you rather questions" here and then answer them as quickly as you can to discover more about yourself!

Would you rather...

Awesome Achievements

Everyone has goals they want to reach.
It doesn't matter how big or small they are.

Keep a list of the things you wish to achieve for the next few weeks. You'll soon discover that even the smallest achievements can measure up to greatness!

EXAMPLES:

- Made my bed for a week
- Raised my hand in class
- Spoke to the new kid at school

I have achieved:

. . . .

. . . .

. . . .

. . . .

. . . .

When you think of something you'd like to do in the future, make a note of it here and see if you can do it!

EXAMPLES:

- Surprising a family member with breakfast in bed
- Passing my piano grading
- Learning how to say ten words in a foreign language

I hope to achieve:

Talent Star

"Everyone has a hidden talent." — SUSAN GALE

Talent isn't just about being able to sing or dance. It can also mean your strengths, like being a problem solver. List your strengths, your friends' strengths and your family's strengths. Then fill in the stars on the opposite page with the names of those who deserve these labels most.

MY STRENGTHS	MY FRIENDS' STRENGTHS	MY FAMILY'S STRENGTHS

Bravest

MOST HONEST

BIGGEST RISK TAKER

QUIRKIEST

Happiest

MOST ATHLETIC

MOST SERIOUS

BRIGHTEST

MOST LOVING

Hardest worker

MOST POLITE

Funniest

BEST HANDWRITING

Life in the Movies

Use the frames below to record your favorite movies of all time, film stars you love to watch, and your own dreams of movie stardom. Write, draw pictures, or glue in pics from magazines.

- Which movie stars do you admire?
- Which characters do you want to be?
- What are your favorite movies?
- What movies do you want to see?
- Keep track of everything in this film reel!

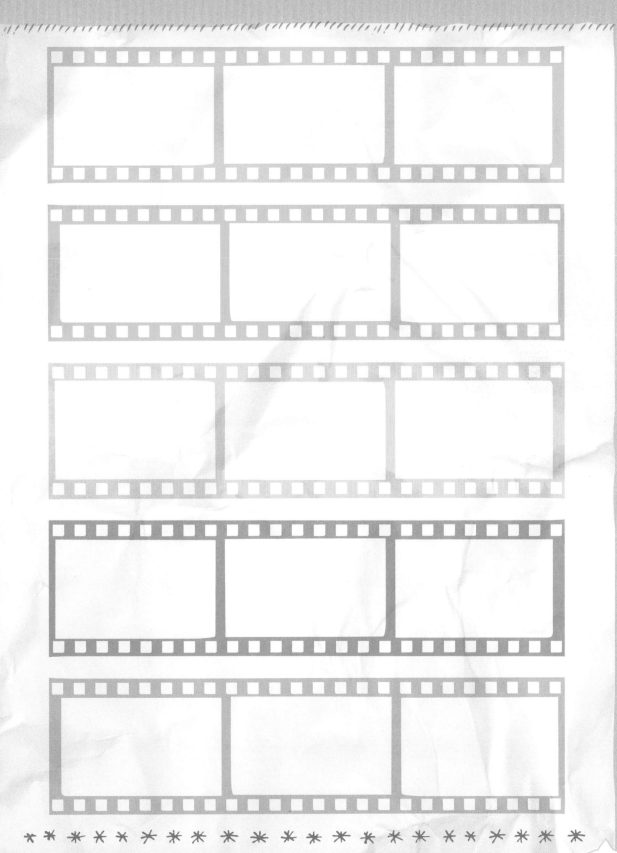

Make School Cool

Everyone moans about
school sometimes,
but why not try to make
things better?

Start by listing the worst thing about
school in each section. Then see if you can
come up with suggestions about how to
tackle the problem. Finally, choose your
best idea and write down what you need
to do next, whether it's talk to a teacher,
get your friends on board, or make
a plan of action.

Lessons

Breaks

Teachers

90

My Dream Vacation

School vacations are the best! Plan your perfect break here.

Will you stay at home or go away?: . . . .

Boarding Pass

Name

From

To

Date

Time

Who is coming with you?

Transport

PACK YOUR SUITCASE (FOR A WEEK) OR BACKPACK (FOR A DAY) WITH:

. . . .

. . . .

. . . .

. . . .

THE WEATHER WILL BE

(circle two answers):

Boiling hot / freezing cold / warm / cool / rainy / sunny / snowy / windy / cloudy

WHERE WILL YOU BE SLEEPING

(circle one answer or write down your own):

My bed / a hammock on the beach / a posh hotel room / a tent / on the floor / a sleepover with friends / a quiet log cabin in the wilderness / other . . .

. . . .

Things you'll eat and drink on vacation:

. . . .

. . . .

. . . .

. . . .

. . . .

LIST THE ACTIVITIES YOU HOPE TO DO:

You could even write a postcard to a friend telling them all about this dream vacation!

ARE THERE ANY SIGHTS YOU MUST SEE?:

. . . .

. . . .

. . . .

. . . .

. . . .

. . . .

. . . .

Home Is Where the Heart Is

Pretend each section of this house represents an area or room in your home.

Write down your favorite parts of each room. Is it the furniture? Or perhaps it's the view out of the window? Maybe it's what happens in the room rather than the things inside it that make it special.

Now dream big and add items to each room to make them even better!

Don't forget the outside areas, or you could always include your local park.

Can you and your family help make any of these dream changes come true?

Let Your Mind Wander

"Either write something worth reading or do something worth writing." — BENJAMIN FRANKLIN

Keep track of the thoughts you have when your mind wanders and you might be surprised by what you come up with.

See anything unusual during the day? Develop a crazy story around it and you'll have given your brain some exercise!

My Q & A

Every time you have a question you don't know the answer to, write it down here then research it later and record the answer.

QUESTIONS AND ANSWERS:

Q _____

_____

A _____

_____

Q _____

_____

A _____

_____

Q _____

_____

A _____

_____

Q _____

_____

A _____

_____

Q _____

_____

A _____

REMINDERS:

1 _____

_____

2 _____

_____

3 _____

_____

WORDS I ALWAYS FORGET HOW TO SPELL:

1 _____   6 _____
2 _____   7 _____
3 _____   8 _____
4 _____   9 _____
5 _____   10 _____

Follow Your Dreams

Make a list of anything and everything you want to do. This list should never end!

And it's never too soon to start checking things off, so why not start today?

Here are some ideas to get you thinking:

- new food to try
- run for student government
- new sporting skills

- improving handwriting
- learning to cartwheel
- places to visit
- books to read

ANYTHING AND EVERYTHING I WANT TO DO:

Love Hearts

What or who do you love? Here's a place to write down everything and everyone that makes your heart sing. Turn to it when you're feeling down and you'll soon remember what makes you smile.

Nearest and Dearest

"It's not WHAT we have in our life, but WHO we have in our life that counts." – J. M. LAURENCE

The people around you are there for fun, friendship, and support! List everyone you know under the three headings on the next page and include photos of some of them. Add a short description or two if you'd like.

MY FAMILY TREE: MY FRIENDSHIP CIRCLE: MY PAW-FECT PETS:

My Famous Family

If you could have a fun celebrity family for a day, who would it include and why?

Add photos of each celebrity from magazines and hashtag reasons why you've chosen them...
#sotalented #amazingsportswoman #givesback

FOLLOW •••

My **celeb mom** would be:

♥ ⚪
∨ ...... LIKES

FOLLOW •••

The **coolest celeb dad** around is:

♥ ⚪
∨ ...... LIKES

FOLLOW •••

Pick four famous people to be your siblings:

♥ ⚪
∨ ...... LIKES

FOLLOW •••

♥ ⚪
∨ ...... LIKES

FOLLOW •••

♥ ⚪
∨ ...... LIKES

FOLLOW •••

♥ ⚪
∨ ...... LIKES

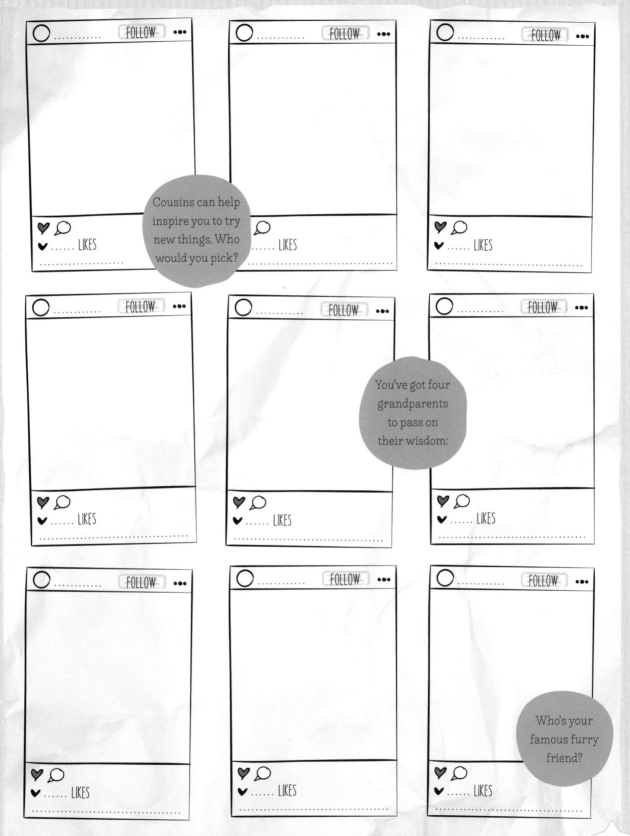

FOLLOW •••
♥ 🗨
♥ ...... LIKES

Cousins can help inspire you to try new things. Who would you pick?

FOLLOW •••
🗨
...... LIKES

FOLLOW •••
♥ 🗨
♥ ...... LIKES

FOLLOW •••
♥ 🗨
♥ ...... LIKES

FOLLOW •••
♥ 🗨
♥ ...... LIKES

You've got four grandparents to pass on their wisdom:

FOLLOW •••
♥ 🗨
♥ ...... LIKES

FOLLOW •••
♥ 🗨
♥ ...... LIKES

FOLLOW •••
♥ 🗨
♥ ...... LIKES

FOLLOW •••
♥ 🗨
♥ ...... LIKES

Who's your famous furry friend?

Fingerprint Friendship Tree

Collect the fingerprints of your family and friends on this friendship tree. Why not make some friendship flowers too?

Just ask everyone to dip their index (the first) finger in some water-soluble paint or ink and watch your foliage burst into life.

Helping Hand

Everyone needs a helping hand sometimes because you never know what might happen in your exciting life. Without thinking about it too hard, jot down who you would want by your side in these situations.

Find a lost kitten with

....

GET MISTAKEN FOR A POP STAR AND MOBBED BY FANS WITH ....

TRY ON NEW SHOES WITH

....

RESEARCH MY FAMILY HISTORY WITH

....

GO FOR A WALK WITH

....

Have a good cry with

....

TRY OUT NEW HAIRSTYLES WITH ....

MAKE CUPCAKES WITH

....

PUT UP PARTY DECORATIONS WITH................................

Go on an around-the-world cruise with ....

PRACTICE DANCE MOVES WITH

....

MEET A TIGER ESCAPED FROM THE ZOO WITH

....

TELL MY DEEPEST SECRETS TO

....

Share the clothes style of

....

DO REALLY HARD HOMEWORK WITH ....

IF I'M SICK, I'D LOVE A VISIT FROM

....

GO FOR A PICNIC WITH

....

ON A RAINY DAY, I WANT TO BE WITH

....

BUILD A TREEHOUSE WITH

....

GO SURFING WITH

....

Birthday Balloons

Keep a note of everyone's birthdays here and you won't be the person who always forgets!

January

February

March

April

May

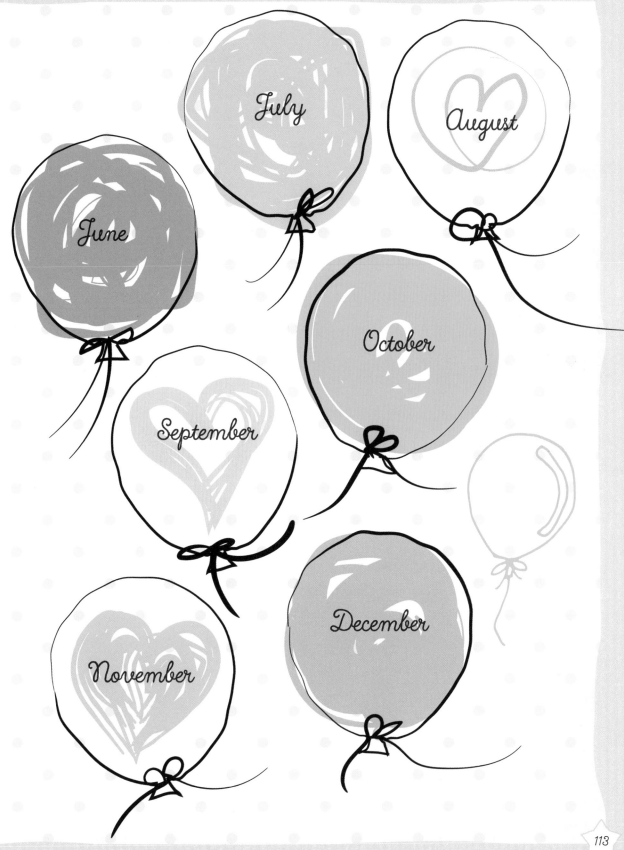

June

July

August

September

October

November

December

Gift to Give

Keep a list of present ideas so you have lots to choose from when a birthday or the holiday season arrives.

WHO?	GIFT IDEA

WHO? GIFT IDEA

Activity Days

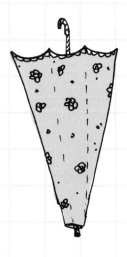

It's always more exciting to go on an adventure with family or do something fun with friends than to sit in front of the TV alone! So why not plan some activities to complete with those you love?

A CRAFT ACTIVITY

WHAT? . . . .

WHO? . . . .

WHERE? . . . .

HOW? . . . .

WHEN? . . . .

AN OUTDOOR ADVENTURE

WHAT? . . . .

WHO? . . . .

WHERE? . . . .

HOW? . . . .

WHEN? . . . .

TRYING SOMETHING NEW

WHAT? . . . . WHO? . . . .

WHERE? . . . . HOW? . . . .

WHEN? . . . .

TREAT TIME

WHAT? . . . . WHO? . . . .

WHERE? . . . . HOW? . . . .

WHEN? . . . .

Tradition Tracker

What are your family traditions? Do you have traditions with friends as well? Do you have a special breakfast for your birthday? Do you stay up for the New Year? Is there something you always do on family vacations? Write down your five favorite traditions!

Example:

Birthdays always begin with breakfast in bed.

Swap, Switch, Share

"The more we share, the more we have."

– LEONARD NIMOY

It's great to share with friends. But keep track of the music, books, and clothes you lend out and you'll avoid any misunderstandings.

ITEM	DATE	BORROWED FROM	DATE RETURNED

ITEM	DATE	LENT TO	DATE RETURNED

SECTION 5

You in Review

HOW LONG HAS IT TAKEN YOU TO FILL IN THIS JOURNAL?

....

WHICH PAGE DID YOU ENJOY THE **MOST**? ....

WHICH PAGE DID YOU FIND THE **HARDEST**? ....

Try to find a word that best describes you for each letter of the alphabet!

A

B

C

D

E

F

G

H

ME
FROM
A TO Z

I

J

K

L

M

N

O

P

Q

R

S

T

U

V

W

X

Y

Z

My Story, My Self

"Tomorrow is another day." – SCARLETT O'HARA

FROM *GONE WITH THE WIND* BY MARGARET MITCHELL

CONGRATULATIONS! You've almost completed your journal. What have you found out about yourself? Complete the sentences below to sum up what you've learned and your hopes for the future.

WHAT HAS SURPRISED ME MOST IS DISCOVERING THAT

. . . .

. . . .

. . . .

. . . .

MY FAMILY IS IMPORTANT TO ME BECAUSE

. . . .

. . . .

. . . .

. . . .

THE BEST THINGS ABOUT MY FRIENDS ARE

. . . .

. . . .

. . . .

I've realized that school is

. . . .

. . . .

. . . .

I WOULDN'T BE WHO I AM TODAY WITHOUT

. . . .

. . . .

. . . .

. . . .

. . . .

. . . .

. . . .

I feel more sure than ever that

. . . .

. . . .

. . . .

. . . .

. . . .

. . . .

. . . .

. . . .

I'M REALLY LOOKING FORWARD TO

. . . .

. . . .

. . . .

. . . .

. . . .

. . . .

. . . .

I'M SO HAPPY I

. . . .

. . . .

. . . .

. . . .

. . . .

. . . .

Time Capsule

If you keep this journal forever, it will act as a time capsule for your future self!

Look back at certain pages from time to time and hopefully you'll be able to check them off as the years go by!

Here are some points in time to get you started, but feel free to add in some more checkpoints.

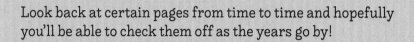

CHECKPOINTS

In two months' time on __ / __ / __
I will look back to pages 62–63 and see if I've had a cozy night in

In six months' time on __ / __ / __
I will check pages 66–67 to see if my music tastes have changed

At the start of the new school year on __ / __ / __
I will see if any changes from pages 90–91 have taken place

In a year's time on __ / __ / __
I will see which items I've crossed off my list from pages 100–101

In five years' time on __ / __ / __
I will see if my sleep style from pages 18–19 has changed

When I move into my own house on __ / __ / __
I will compare my bedroom to my dream room from pages 22–23

CHECKPOINTS

My Story, My Self

Every day the sun rises and you get a full 24 hours of life to enjoy! What does today have in store for you?

Be happy!

Find a favorite photo and put it in the frame, or draw a picture of your smiling face to remind you how great you are!

First edition for the United States, its territories and dependencies, and Canada published in 2018 by Barron's Educational Series, Inc.

Published in 2018 by Carlton Books Limited, an imprint of the Carlton Publishing Group, 20 Mortimer Street, London, W1T 3JW

Text, design, and illustration copyright © Carlton Books Limited 2018

All inquiries should be addressed to:
Barron's Educational Series, Inc.
250 Wireless Boulevard
Hauppauge, NY 11788
www.barronseduc.com

ISBN: 978-1-4380-1148-6

Date of manufacture: January 2018
Manufactured by: RR Donnelley, Dongguan, China

Printed in China

9 8 7 6 5 4 3 2 1

Author: Anna Brett
Executive Editor: Alexandra Koken
Design Manager: Emily Clarke
Design: Rachel Lawston
Production: Emma Smart

Illustrations by Pheobe Leadbeater and Shutterstock